Decisions, decisions

A Lent study course

NICK FAWCETT

First published in 2000 by
KEVIN MAYHEW LTD
Buxhall
Stowmarket
Suffolk IP14 3BW

0 1 2 3 4 5 6 7 8 9

ISBN 1 84003 665 6
Catalogue No 1500403

Cover design by Jonathan Stroulger
Edited by Katherine Laidler
Typesetting by Louise Selfe
Printed and bound in Great Britain

Contents

*To all those of many Christian traditions
who have helped shape my own journey of faith*

Introduction

How good are you at making decisions? Are you the sort who takes the bull by the horns and tackles a situation head on, or the type who prevaricates, constantly putting off decisions until tomorrow? Whether it's moving house or applying for a new job, choosing an outfit or making up one's mind about some controversial issue, it's much easier to keep one's options open, to postpone a decision until another day. Sometimes that can be down to laziness, but not always. In many areas of life, especially those most important to us, it can be hard to know just how we ought to decide; while in other areas, though we know what we should do, it takes courage to do it. Afraid of making the wrong decision, we end up making no decision at all. That may not matter, or it may matter very much, for some decisions will shape the rest of our lives.

So how do we choose? Is it merely a question of asking God for guidance and then doing his will? Occasionally that may be the case, but life is rarely quite so straightforward. Many issues are bewildering in their complexity and, though the Scriptures can often help, sometimes there is little concrete guidance on offer; the onus is on us to come to a decision. Of course, God promises his help to all who seek his will, but finally we must decide; he cannot do it for us. That may not be comfortable, but it is the essence of free will, and also the essence of Lent. Like Jesus in the wilderness, we must wrestle with the issues of life and the challenge of faith.

The five sessions in this book explore different aspects of life's decisions, each drawing upon biblical passages and personal experiences. They do not even begin to exhaust the subject, but rather suggest avenues for further discussion. The material is set out as follows:

- Each session begins with a traditional prayer, followed by a short paragraph introducing the overall theme.
- After this, a fun element (activity) is brought in, using group games or quizzes. These activities will not only help break the

ice but also encourage informal reflection on the issues covered in the study. Note that they will need some preparation beforehand (see page 47). You will probably be able to get hold of the recommended game/resource from among your friends, family or other members of the group. If not, try inventing your own substitute! Although I have suggested items for discussion here, don't get bogged down in deep debate; the time for a fuller discussion will come later. This whole section should be kept to a maximum of 15 minutes.

- Next comes a Bible passage (my own paraphrase). This should be read aloud by the group leader, or one of the group members – provided that they have been given time to prepare beforehand. Avoid asking people to read on the spot – some may not come again if you do so.

- The 'Comment' section that follows the reading is not designed for reading in a group context. Ideally, participants should study it before the meeting. Alternatively, allow a few minutes of quiet at this point so that everyone can read it at their own pace.

- Sum up the key points using the 'Summary' section and invite people's thoughts on the subject so far.

- Allow discussion to develop and introduce into this the questions provided.

- You may also like to bring in the passages suggested for further reading at this point; alternatively, leave these for group members to reflect on at home.

- After allowing ample time for discussion, use the meditation to draw people's thoughts together, and then, briefly, outline the suggestions for action. Invite any further ideas from the group.

- Finally, end the meeting in prayer, using either the prayer provided or your own.

It is my hope that this study may help us as individuals and in small groups to reflect on the challenge of Lent and the decisions God calls us to make.

Nick Fawcett

First week of Lent

A time to decide

Prayer

Give to me, Lord, a steadfast heart,
    which no unworthy affection may drag downwards;
    give me an unconquered heart,
    which no tribulation can wear out;
    give me an upright heart,
    which no unworthy purpose may tempt aside.
Bestow upon me, also, O Lord God,
    understanding to know you,
    diligence to seek you,
    wisdom to find you
    and a faithfulness that may finally embrace you.
Amen.

Thomas Aquinas

Introduction

Should we buy it or shouldn't we? It was a difficult decision. We'd fallen in love with the house at first sight, but there were a lot of questions to be sorted. Could we afford it? Was it too far out of town? Would there be enough room for us as well as space for a much-needed study? We were torn between what our hearts and our heads were telling us. Eventually we put in an offer but, unsurprisingly, it was turned down. It had to be the full price or nothing. So we were back where we started, going round and round in circles as we mulled over the problem, assessing whether we could stretch ourselves that little bit further. So what did we do? The answer may not surprise you. It was to sleep on it for a few more days; to go away on the holiday we had planned and see how we felt when we got back. A sound policy, would you say? Or was it simply a way of ducking the issue?

We did decide eventually. The attraction was too strong, so, throwing caution to the wind, we dashed round to the estate agent on our return, hoping to seal the deal. Only we were too late; the house had gone, another bid accepted the night before. Funnily enough, it was probably for the best, the house impractical for our purposes, but the principle is clear enough. Put off a decision and you may find, when you do finally make up your mind, that it's too late – the decision taken out of your hands. For us all there comes a time to decide.

Activity
Jenga, Kerplunk or Matchsticks (see page 47).

Reading: Mark 1:1-11
The gospel of Jesus Christ; how it all started. In the words of the prophet Isaiah: 'Look, I am sending my messenger before you, who will prepare your way; a voice crying in the wilderness, "Prepare the way of the Lord, make his paths straight."' So John came, baptising in the wilderness, proclaiming a baptism of repentance for the forgiveness of sins. And from all Judea and Jerusalem, people went out to him, and, confessing their sins, were baptised in the River Jordan. He was clothed with camel's hair, wore a leather belt around his waist, and ate locusts and wild honey. He proclaimed, 'There is one greater than I coming after me; I have no right even to bend down and loosen the thong of his sandals. I have baptised you with water, but he will baptise you with the Holy Spirit.'

Then Jesus came from Nazareth, in Galilee, and was baptised by John in the Jordan. And, as he came up out of the water, he saw the heavens burst open and the Spirit falling like a dove upon him. And a voice sounded from heaven, 'You are my beloved Son; with you I am well pleased.'

Comment

'Then Jesus came from Nazareth, in Galilee, and was baptised by John in the Jordan.' So Mark introduces the beginning of the ministry of Jesus. It is easy to assume that this must have been one of the most joyful events in his life, an occasion which everything thus far had been building up to, but was it? How easy a decision must it actually have been for Jesus to leave his home in Nazareth and set off for the Jordan, there to take his first step on the road to the cross? We need to remember that Jesus was aged around thirty when this moment came – thirty years in which, presumably, he had lived a quiet and unremarkable life pursuing the trade of his father. How did he feel when news of John the Baptist's preaching reached him and he realised that his hour had come? Did his spirit leap with excitement, or recoil in fear? Was this a moment he'd been looking forward to, or a time he'd been dreading? We will never know. What we do know, however, is this: that Jesus answered the call. He went out into the wilderness to be baptised and so set in motion the three years of his ministry that cost him so much. His hour had come: a time to decide.

It wasn't only Jesus, though, who had to make up his mind; it was everyone. The multitude who flocked to hear John the Baptist preaching – each of them was challenged to turn from their old way of life and start again. Then others, only this time put on the spot not by John but by Jesus. First Peter, Andrew, James and John, out for a spot of fishing, when suddenly a stranger confronted them with the words, 'Follow me'. Then Matthew, sitting in his tax-collector's booth, and again the same challenge: 'Follow me'. And so it was to continue – to a rich young man seeking eternal life: 'Sell everything that you have and give the money to the poor';

to a woman caught in the act of adultery: 'Go and sin no more'; to a paralysed man by the Pool of Siloam: 'Do you want to be made well?' Repeatedly the story was the same: those who met with Jesus found that the hour had come for them too; a time to decide.

In similar fashion, it comes to us today. At different times and in different ways God puts us on the spot and calls for our response. For some it might be the challenge to commit their life to Christ, with the attendant questions that brings: Am I ready to follow? Am I sure of my faith? Do I understand what I'm taking on? For others it might be the call to service or a position of leadership; while for others still it might mean a change of lifestyle, an acknowledgement of mistakes, or a resolve to begin again. It might be something large or something small; a decision which changes the entire course of one's life or which simply influences one small aspect. Shall I go to church or stay at home and wash the car? Shall I stand up for what I believe or turn a blind eye? Shall I make time for prayer and devotion or shall I get that odd job done round the house? Shall I brood over past wrongs or act as peacemaker? Shall I speak of my faith or keep quiet? Shall I give sacrificially or look after number one?

We can, of course, continue to push such questions aside, hoping they'll go away. We can tell ourselves that we'll get to them all in good time, when there are less pressing matters to concern ourselves with. We can go on postponing a decision to another day, just as we have done so many times before, but we will find no peace that way; we will simply condemn ourselves to struggle on with the burden of that unresolved question. What we need to do is to consider what is being asked of us and who is doing the asking. Is it simply our own ideas, or is it the voice of God, urging us forward, calling us to respond in faith? If it's the latter, then there's one more question we need not only to ask but also to answer: isn't it time to decide?

Summary

- Few decisions are easy. Many can have life-changing implications.
- The ministries of John the Baptist and Jesus both demanded a response.
- All of us face decisions, large and small.
- We can't run away from decisions for ever. Finally, they need to be faced.
- Postponing a decision is counterproductive. The knowledge that we still have to make a decision can weigh heavily upon us, destroying our peace of mind.
- Is God calling us to make a decision? What is it? Is it time we made our choice?

Discussion

- In the early 1980s, when the home computer was being developed, several leading firms, including the giant IBM company, felt that the technology had no future. They waited to see how things would develop before committing themselves to a decision. Twenty years on, with Microsoft dominating the market, several are ruing their failure to act. Have there been times in your experience when putting off a decision proved costly? In what way? Why did you put off making a decision? Were you able to undo any of the damage caused by your delay?
- Are there decisions you have made which have changed your life for the better? What were they? What helped you in making up your mind?
- Are there times when you have made a decision you thought was right but which turned out to be wrong? What do you think caused things to work out the way they did?
- What decisions in life do you find hardest? Is there anything you are putting off because you would rather not face it?

- Are you conscious of God's call but unsure what he is asking you to do?
- How would you approach a difficult decision? Who or what would you find most helpful in enabling you to make it? Where would you look to first for God's guidance?

Meditation

Time to decide?
Come off it, what's the rush?
There's ages yet,
    no hurry.
I want to live a little first,
    let my hair down and enjoy myself.
You're only young once, after all –
    time for the serious stuff later.

Time to decide?
Not yet, Lord –
    tomorrow will do.
I'm busy right now,
    no time to stop –
    come back another day.
You understand, don't you?
It's not that I don't want to listen,
    but there's the house, the garden, the job, the family –
    so much to do and so little time to do it –
    I'll get round to you eventually, I promise.

Time to decide?
I'm frightened, Lord –
    scared of what you might ask,
    what committing myself might involve.
I don't like to say no,
    but I'm terrified of saying yes,

so give me a little longer,
    just a few more days.
Please!

Time to decide?
Do I have to?
I'm happy with the way things are,
    quite content to plod along –
    why go upsetting the applecart?
Let's leave it for now, shall we? –
    wait until the moment's right.
You don't mind, do you?

Time to decide?
Fair enough, Lord, I'm ready.
What was that?
Too late!
The decision made.
I don't understand what you mean.
Lord, I'm listening,
    I'm ready!
Lord?

Further reading
Matthew 11:28-30; Luke 9:57-62; Acts 26:1-23

Suggestions for action
Stop putting off important decisions this week. Meet them head on and resolve them. If you feel God is calling you in some way but you need more guidance, talk things through with a friend or your minister. If you're convinced you know what God is calling you to do, stop thinking about it; do it!

Prayer

Living God,
    you do not force us to decide;
    instead, you invite our response.
You do not dictate what we should do,
    rather you want us to make up our own minds.
You are always there,
    calling,
    coaxing,
    guiding,
    prompting,
    but ultimately you leave decisions up to us.
Save us from running away from that challenge,
    from putting off until tomorrow
    what we know should be tackled today,
    and save us too from evading your call,
    afraid of what it may involve.
Help us to listen for your voice and seek your will,
    and, having done that as best we can,
    give us the wisdom and courage we need to decide wisely.
In the name of Christ we ask it.
Amen.

Second week of Lent

Complex decisions

Prayer

O gracious and holy Father,
  give us wisdom to perceive you,
  intelligence to understand you,
  diligence to seek you,
  patience to wait for you,
  eyes to behold you,
  a heart to meditate upon you
  and a life to proclaim you,
  through the power of the Spirit of Jesus Christ our Lord.
Amen.

St Benedict

Introduction

What is the difference between 'forgo' and 'forego'? Do you know?
It's surprising how many people don't, the two words frequently
used as if they are interchangeable. In fact, 'forgo' means 'to give
up or relinquish', whereas 'forego' means 'to precede'. The words
may appear similar but they signify something very different. So
how about two other words, also looking very much alike: 'premiss'
and 'premise' – what's the difference this time? The answer is that
there isn't one: both terms mean exactly the same thing! Which you
use this time is entirely a matter of personal preference. Confusing,
isn't it! Yet no more confusing than many other decisions we have to
make throughout our lives. Though choices may often be straightforward, at other times they may be anything but, some issues so
complex we do not know what to make of them. So does it matter?

Should we adopt a policy of live and let live, and have done with it? Are all moral judgements necessarily relative? Or, despite the bewildering array of options sometimes open to us, is there a right way forward for us to take?

Activity
Call My Bluff, Scruples or the Balloon Game (see page 47).

Reading: Matthew 4:1-11

Then Jesus was led into the wilderness by the Spirit to be tempted by the devil, and, having fasted there for forty days and nights, he was famished. Then the tempter approached him and said, 'If you are the Son of God, tell these stones to become loaves of bread.' But he answered, 'It is written, "We do not live by bread alone, but by every word that comes from the mouth of God."' Then the devil took him to the holy city and, placing him on the pinnacle of the temple, he said to him, 'If you are the Son of God, hurl yourself down from here, for it is written, "He will order his angels to watch over you", and "their hands will support you, lest you shatter your foot against a stone."' Jesus said to him, 'Again it is written, "You shall not test the Lord your God."' Yet once more the devil came, and took him up to a lofty mountaintop where he showed him all the kingdoms of the world in all their glory; and he said to him, 'If you will bow down and worship me I will give you all these.' Jesus said to him, 'Get away from me, Satan! for it is written, "You shall worship the Lord your God, and shall serve only him."' Then the devil left him, and at once angels came and waited on him.

Comment

A few weeks ago I received a phone call from the *Baptist Times* asking me if I would contribute a comment to their regular current affairs slot. The question put to me concerned an issue very much in the news at the time: 'The Human Genome Project – does it chill or thrill?' So how did I answer? Did I applaud this venture as a groundbreaking initiative, or did I condemn it, as so many seem to, as a presumptuous attempt to play God? Surprise, surprise, I did neither! My reply, instead, was a hybrid of the two: a cautious welcome of the possibilities such research opens up, coupled with an expression of concern over the ethical dilemmas it inevitably poses.

Many, reading my response, may have felt I chose to sit on the fence, preferring to play safe rather than make a definite stand, but I would dispute that. The question put me in mind of my schooldays and the introduction during that time of multiple choice examinations. At the time, they seemed like a godsend. No more sitting in front of a blank piece of paper, racking one's brains for inspiration – the answer to every question was there on the examination paper, and if seeing it in black and white failed to jog the memory there was always the possibility of selecting it by default. Yet, somehow, it didn't quite turn out to be that simple, for the examiners were no fools. Occasionally one of the answers offered was blatantly wrong, but very rarely so. Most of them looked deceptively right. Selecting the correct response from the various options was by no means the doddle I'd anticipated; in fact, often the choice given served to confuse rather than enlighten. So it was with that question put to me by the *Baptist Times*, and so it is in innumerable areas of life. Good and evil, right and wrong, are not always black and white, much though we might wish they were. More often than not, they are a murky shade of grey.

Is that difficulty in understanding down to us, a sign of our fatally flawed human nature? It may be, but not necessarily. On the contrary, it may be a sign of maturity rather than weakness, for some decisions are anything but simple. Look, for example, at the temptations faced by Jesus. Were the issues he faced straightforward, or did he have a variety of options from which to choose? Today, with the benefit of hindsight, we can all too easily regard that time in the wilderness as a mere formality, his ultimate triumph a *fait accompli*, but to imagine that is to miss the point entirely. For the issues put before Jesus were by no means a simple matter of rejecting what was obviously wrong and choosing what was evidently right. Like my multiple choice questions, the examination he faced was much more subtle and far more demanding.

Take the first suggestion put to him: 'If you are the Son of God, turn these stones into bread.' What was wrong with that? It all sounds innocuous enough. Why shouldn't he satisfy his hunger? Why not make the most of his gifts? Hadn't God given them to him for a reason? Anyway, there was no one around, so who was to know? It couldn't do any harm, surely.

Then there was the second temptation: Jesus taken up onto the temple and urged to throw himself down so that he could assure himself of God's protection. Was that so terrible? Here was the chance to prove, not only to himself but also to others, that God was with him. Surely that would win over the sceptics? And, let's face it, much was being asked of Jesus, a challenge far greater than any of us would ever expect to bear, so why not seek all the reassurances he could get?

'Ah,' you may say, 'but how about the final temptation, that challenge from Satan: "Bow down and worship me, and all this will be yours"? Not much doubt this time, is there?' Or is there? We need to dig a bit deeper and ask what was actually going on here, for somehow I don't think Jesus was confronted by a strange creature with horns and a forked tail! It was rather that he wrestled with the temptation to tone down his message and play it safe. Why not compromise a little if it made people more sympathetic to his cause? Why not turn a blind eye occasionally if doing so avoided alienating those very people he was trying to reach? Why worry too much about a spiritual kingdom when he could establish one on earth there and then? Bow to Satan? – of course not; but bend with the wind – which of us hasn't done that?

All this is not to suggest that there wasn't a right or a wrong way, for there clearly was. What I'm saying is that the issues were not as clear as we might like to think, so much so that even Scripture could be taken and twisted out of context so that the ends justified the means. The temptations faced by Jesus were real, the issues he wrestled with complex and the suggestions put before him subtle – not a series of patently shocking insinuations but rather an assortment of questions concerning the future and his willingness to grasp it. What was he letting himself in for? Had God really called him to walk the path of suffering and sacrifice, or was there some easier way? He had to distinguish between what *could* be and what *should* be the way ahead; to listen to the arguments and then measure them against what he believed God was saying about his future ministry. This was no brief sortie into the wilderness to rubber-stamp conclusions already reached. It was a long and demanding time of soul-searching; a testing examination that was to dictate the course of his life and, to get through it, he needed not a set of rules but a direct and intimate relationship with God.

Such an approach does not come easily to us. We like to know where we stand, to have clear guidelines, the parameters between right and wrong clearly marked. So it was with the scribes and Pharisees. 'Why does your teacher eat with tax collectors and sinners?' (Matthew 9:11). 'Is it lawful to heal on the Sabbath?' (Matthew 12:9). 'Why do your disciples flout the tradition of the elders?' (Matthew 15:2). 'Why does this man speak like this? It is blasphemy! Surely only God can forgive sins?' (Mark 2:7). They knew what God wanted. It was set out in the law, a right answer for every occasion. What right had Jesus to challenge that authority? Allow him to do that and who could say where it would end? But the way of Christ is very different from any other; a way that can be summed up in one simple instruction: 'This is my commandment, that you love one another as I have loved you' (John 15:12).

It's not easy, living by the yardstick of love. There are some who will tell you that it is wishy-washy and woolly, fogging the issue and inviting an 'anything goes' attitude. Some will prefer instead to hide behind the security of rules and regulations, insisting on a world of moral absolutes. It may be more comfortable to do that, but it doesn't make it right. Life isn't neat and tidy, however much we might wish it were, so why should faith be any different? Lent

19

invites us to spend time reflecting on that faith, not alone, but with God's help. It calls us to make room for him, to reflect on his word and seek his will, so that when choices need to be made, he will help us to make them.

Summary

- Decisions are rarely straightforward. Often they involve complex issues and many sides to the argument.
- For Jesus, too, decisions were complicated. The time he faced in the wilderness involved genuine and difficult choices.
- Discerning God's will is not always a matter of clear-cut decisions. It can be hard to find biblical guidance relating to controversial issues in the news today. Even where guidance is given, we can consciously or unconsciously twist its meaning – the devil can use Scripture for his own ends.
- We can use the complexity of issues as an excuse for ducking them or for watering down our response.
- The opponents of Jesus accused him of moral laxity for his apparent flouting of the law and tradition.
- There *are* rights and wrongs, but we cannot encapsulate these through a set of laws. Faith involves walking the way of love, even though the path may seem anything but clear.

Discussion

- Much in the news recently has been the issue of fuel. Should the price come down? If so, how should the government fund public services like health and education? Would you be happy to see such services cut? Is road tax a better solution to raising funds, or does this penalise those who only travel a little or use public transport? Should the price of fuel be kept high in an effort to reduce the emission of greenhouse gases? (Don't expect to find definitive answers to such questions, still less fall out over them. As with most issues, there are valid arguments on both sides.)

- What contentious areas do you find it hard to reach a decision about? Do you think there can be a united Christian voice concerning such matters? Should there be?

- Have there been times when you had to revise your opinions as to what is right and wrong? What issues were involved? What caused you to think again?

- Are there two sides to every question? If so, what are the implications for Christian morality? In what way should it shape our decisions?

- Is openness to questions a sign of faith or doubt?

- Is openness to different points of view a sign of strength or weakness?

Meditation

I'm trying to decide, Lord,
  believe me, I'm trying,
  and if you'd asked me yesterday
  I'd have said I'd succeeded,
  my mind made up,
  the debate over.
Only I couldn't escape that little voice in my head,
  refusing to be silenced,
  insisting that there was more to the matter
  than I'd allowed.
I tried to ignore it, but it was no good,
  for, unfortunately, it was true,
  the more I stopped to consider,
  the more complicated I saw the issue was.

There weren't just two sides to the argument but many,
   each with their pros and cons,
   their good and their bad points,
   and instead of leading me towards an answer,
   they took me further away,
   my head suddenly spinning with uncertainty.
I wish I could go back to how it used to be –
   everything straightforward,
   cut and dried,
   for it was easy that way,
   no need to think for myself,
   in fact, no real decision to take;
   but I realise now that life isn't like that,
   not neat and tidy,
   not simple or straightforward at all.
I can't say I like it, Lord,
   wrestling with choices,
   accepting that what I thought was right
   may turn out to be wrong,
   but if I'm serious about finding answers,
   not mine but yours,
   then I need first to face the questions,
   and to listen to what you are saying to me there.

Feb 17th AM

Gen 2 : 15-17 3 : 1-7
Ps 32
Rom 5 : 12-19
Matt 4 : 1-11

1st Sun Lent.

Further reading
1 Kings 3:16-28; Matthew 22:15-22

Suggestions for action
Are there judgements you have made without considering the facts?
If so, reconsider the issues involved and ask yourself if you have
come to the right decision. Ask God for help to be open and fair-
minded, while at the same time staying true to your convictions.

Prayer

Living God,
    day by day we have to choose,
    to make decisions about right and wrong,
    good and evil.
Sometimes the choice is clear, sometimes confusing;
    sometimes easy, sometimes hard;
    sometimes mattering little, sometimes much,
    but, whatever the case,
    we have the responsibility to seek your will
    and to make up our minds
    as to the best way forward.
Help us to decide wisely,
    for there is so much we do not understand,
    so many complicated and confusing areas of life.
Grant us faith to wrestle with such matters,
    confident that you can use them
    to lead us to new insights
    and a deeper awareness of your sovereign purpose.
Teach us to be honest with you
    and open to all that you would say to us,
    and so may we grow in faith and understanding,
    to the glory of your name.
Through Jesus Christ our Lord.
Amen.

Third week of Lent

Who decides?

Prayer

Lord God,
    light of the minds that know you,
    life of the souls that love you,
    strength of the wills that serve you,
    help us so to know you that we may truly love you
    and so to love you that we may fully serve you,
    whose service is perfect freedom;
    through Jesus Christ our Lord.
Amen.

Gelasian Sacramentary

Introduction

The notice was clear enough: ROAD CLOSED. Normally, we'd have turned back straightaway and taken an alternative route, but that day we were in a hurry, a deadline rapidly approaching, and, besides that, plenty of motorists seemed to be ignoring the warning and driving straight on. Perhaps they knew something we didn't. Even more convincing was the fact that traffic was flowing freely from the opposite direction. Clearly something was getting through. Should we risk it? All right, just this once. So, following the lead of cars ahead of us, we carried on; and a good thing too, we decided, as the next mile passed swiftly without incident. But then, out of the blue, a car in front veered sharply, and a succession of feet slammed down on the brakes. It was chaos – traffic coming at us from two directions and nowhere for us to go but back the way we came. We returned sadder and wiser for the experience.

It was foolish, of course, but a fair illustration of human nature. We like to think we know best, don't we, never mind what the authorities tell us. So often, until we've seen and tried something for ourselves, we won't be satisfied and, in consequence, we so often end up learning the hard way. Undeniably, there are times when we need to think for ourselves but, equally, there are occasions when we need the humility to take advice on trust. Ironically, that can be hardest decision of all.

Activity

Lego (see page 47).

Reading: Joshua 24:14-18

Honour the Lord, and offer him true and faithful service. Renounce the gods that your ancestors served beyond the Euphrates and in Egypt, and serve the Lord. If you would rather not serve the Lord, then choose this day whom you will serve, whether the gods your ancestors served in the region beyond the Euphrates or the gods of the Amorites in whose land you are living; but as for me and my household, we will serve the Lord.' Then the people answered, 'Forsake the Lord to serve other gods? That's the last thing we'd do; for it was the Lord our God who delivered us and our people from slavery in Egypt and who did those great signs in our sight. He protected us throughout our journey from all the people through whose lands we passed; and he drove the Amorites and all the inhabitants of the land out before us. Therefore we too will serve the Lord, for he is our God.'

Comment

'I did it my way!' So say the words of the classic song immortalised by Frank Sinatra, and for many that simple phrase sums up their approach to life. Never mind what other people say or think; they are going to live as they see fit, to follow their own rules, no one else's.

So is that right or wrong? The answer, of course, as in so much in life, is a bit of both. We expect to make our own decisions, we regard freedom of conscience and expression as our right, and we believe it is up to us rather than someone else to choose how we spend our time. All of this is part of the liberty we justifiably prize and it would be a sorry day should we ever lose it. Besides, it is important that we accept responsibility for our actions, not hiding behind others or being swept along by the crowd, but standing on our own two feet, thinking and deciding for ourselves.

Yet, Lent reminds us that there is another dimension to life, another factor in the equation – one that we see anticipated centuries back in the days of Joshua: 'Choose this day whom you will serve'; words which challenged the people to make up their minds, to decide once and for all where their allegiance lay. Will they serve themselves and their own interests? Will they worship the gods others worship, gods of their own making? Or will they accept that there is a higher authority, sovereign over heaven and earth, one to whom all finally owe allegiance? More important still, will they accept that truth not just with their minds but their hearts, allowing it to shape their lives and control their actions?

Here is the challenge at the heart of Lent; the challenge that Jesus wrestled with at the start of his ministry and which he called others to wrestle with in turn. Of course, we've done our bit through confessing our faith and Christ as Lord, or have we? Is that sufficient? Is that really all Jesus asks of us? Consider, for a moment, the experience of Simon Peter:

> *Coming into the vicinity of Caesarea Philippi, Jesus asked his disciples, 'Who do people say that the Son of Man is?' They answered, 'Some say John the Baptist, others Elijah, others Jeremiah or one of the prophets.' He said to them, 'But what about you – who do you say that I am?' Simon Peter answered, 'You are the Christ, the Son of the living God.'*
> (Matthew 16:13-16)

Here was a moment when it looked for all the world as though Peter had understood who Jesus was, what his coming meant and continues to mean, what he had come to do – and, to be fair, he had grasped a lot more than his fellow Apostles. Yet the conversation that followed betrays how much he still had to learn:

> From that point onwards, Jesus began to teach his disciples that he needed to go to Jerusalem and suffer many things at the hands of the elders, chief priests and scribes; that he would be killed, and on the third day raised to life. Taking him to one side, Peter began to admonish him, saying, 'Heaven help us, Lord! This mustn't be allowed to happen.' Then Jesus turned on Peter and said, 'Get behind me, Satan! You are blocking my path; for you are seeing things from a human perspective rather than the way God sees them.' (Matthew 16:21-23)

It's hard not to feel sorry for Peter, for which of us in his shoes wouldn't have felt and probably spoken precisely as he did? How could anyone kill a man like Jesus? How could the promised deliverer suffer and die? How could God possibly let it happen? It just didn't make sense. And, of course, in human terms he was quite right, for how could a man hung up on a cross and sealed in a tomb hope to make a difference to anyone, let alone transform the destiny of the world? Yet, as Jesus so neatly put it, to think like that is to set our minds not on divine but human things; to join in the refrain 'I did it my way' rather than 'I did it God's way'.

Lent urges us to be different: to look at the world not simply with our own eyes but with God's; to look at life and to recognise that he is able to work there in ways beyond our imagining. It means saying to him, as Jesus was able to say, 'Not my will but yours be done.' Can we do that? We may think so, but is it truly God's way we follow or our own, his way or that of others? It's easy to deceive ourselves and follow our own inclinations. It's easy to be taken in by others and to follow the crowd. To take a conscious decision to seek God's will and follow the way of Christ takes faith, humility and courage. Are we ready to take that step?

Summary

- We need to make our own decisions but that doesn't mean we must do everything our own way.
- The people of Israel in the time of Joshua had to decide whose way they would follow: their own or God's.
- Peter believed he had made his decision to follow Jesus but events were to prove him wrong. He had to learn that his way and God's way were not the same.
- God's way does not always appear to make sense but we need the faith of Jesus to say, 'Not my will but yours be done.'
- We can be enticed into following our own way or the way of the crowd, sometimes fooling ourselves into thinking it is what God wants of us. Lent is a time for study and reflection, designed to help us discover God's will.

Discussion

- Several athletes in recent years have followed the celebrated example of Eric Liddell in refusing to compete on a Sunday. What do you make of their decision? Other Christian sportspeople regularly now take part in Sunday events, just as numerous Christians find themselves having to work on Sundays. How do we feel about this situation?
- In what ways does God speak to us? How far can we know his will?
- Friends of mine believed themselves called to the mission field and, after training, set off full of enthusiasm. They returned a few years later, bitterly disillusioned by their experiences and convinced missionary work wasn't for them. What can cause us to confuse God's will with our own?
- Are there situations today when we have to choose between the world's way and God's way? What pressures from society most threaten to compromise our convictions?

- Are we serious when we say, 'Your will be done'?
- What holds us back from allowing God freedom to direct our decisions and shape our lives? How would you answer someone else's concerns?

Meditation

'Your will be done,
   on earth as it is in heaven.'
Yes, I know I said it, Lord,
   but I didn't expect you to take me literally;
   never imagined for a moment you'd hold me to the bargain.
Change the world by all means,
   others too, come to that,
   but me? –
   can't you make an exception?
What I meant by 'Your will be done'
   was 'Let it be your will',
   not 'If it be'.
Come on, Lord, be reasonable.
You know best, I realise that,
   and of course your purpose comes first,
   but surely you can work round me,
   fit my requests into your plan somewhere?
That's not too much to ask, is it?
You know what I want from you,
   how much it means to me –
   don't go spoiling things, please.
What's that you say?
I've got things wrong,
   my priorities muddled?
Now hang on, Lord,
   I've said it once,
   I'll say it again,

'Not your will but mine be done.'
Whoops, I got that wrong, didn't I?
Didn't I?

Further reading

Genesis 3:1-6; Deuteronomy 30:11-20; Matthew 7:21-27

Suggestions for action

Identify an area in your life where you know you are resisting
God's will in preference to your own. Examine your motives and
pray for help in changing. Strive this week to follow his way.

Prayer

Sovereign God,
    we want to echo the words of Jesus:
    'Not my will but yours be done',
    but we find it so hard to put you first and self second.
Despite our promises of allegiance,
    we expect you to accommodate our wishes
    and bow to our demands,
    and, when you fail to deliver the goods,
    we wonder why you have not answered our prayer.
We speak of seeking your guidance
    and discovering your purpose,
    yet, more often than not, we trust in *our* judgement,
    our minds already made up before we approach you.

Open our hearts to your presence
and give us humility to listen,
wisdom to understand
and faith to follow.
Help us to say, 'Your will be done',
and to mean it!
In Christ's name we ask it.
Amen.

Fourth week of Lent

Flawed decisions

Prayer

Grant me, Lord,
>to know what I ought to know,
>to love what I ought to love,
>to praise what delights you most,
>to value what is precious in your sight,
>and to hate what is offensive to you.

Let me not judge according to superficial appearances,
>nor condemn on the basis of what others say;
>but may I have the discernment
>to understand deeper realities,
>and above all to seek your will.

Amen.

Thomas à Kempis

Introduction

Fans of *Fawlty Towers* will never forget the classic episode when a German couple arrive to stay at the hotel. Terrified of putting his foot in it, Basil Fawlty warns his staff, 'Don't mention the war', only to refer to it himself repeatedly! It's an hilarious spoof, but sadly all too often life can be like that, our prejudices surfacing despite ourselves, colouring all our attitudes and shaping the way we perceive the world. It is tempting to imagine we are different – open-minded, tolerant, unbiased – but I doubt that is true of any of us. We are all inevitably shaped by our past, developing our own set of preconceptions as we go through life. Today we explore the implications of that in terms of the decisions we make concerning those around us; and, specifically, we reflect on the danger of passing judgement in the light of those invariably flawed decisions.

Activity

Optical illusions (see page 48).

Reading: 1 Samuel 16:1-13

The Lord said to Samuel, 'How much longer are you going to lament over Saul? I have rejected him as king over Israel. Fill your horn with oil and get moving; I want you to go to Jesse in Bethlehem, for I have chosen one of his sons to be king.' Samuel said, 'How can I do that? Saul will kill me if he gets to hear of it.' The Lord answered, 'Take a heifer with you, and say you have come to offer a sacrifice to the Lord. Invite Jesse to the sacrifice, and I will show you what you shall do; anoint the one I show you.' Samuel followed the Lord's instructions, and went to Bethlehem. The elders of the city hurried anxiously to greet him, asking 'Why are you here? Do you come in peace?' 'In peace,' said Samuel. 'I have come to sacrifice to the Lord; sanctify yourselves and come with me to the sacrifice.' He personally sanctified Jesse and his sons and invited them to attend the sacrifice as well.

They came, and the moment he spotted Eliab he thought, 'This must be the one God has chosen to be anointed.' But the Lord said to Samuel, 'Don't be taken in by good looks or physique, because I have rejected him. The Lord does not see as people see, for they look at appearances, but the Lord sees into the heart.' Then Jesse called Abinadab, and made him pass before Samuel, but he said, 'No, this isn't the Lord's chosen one.' Then Jesse presented Shammah, but again Samuel said, 'No, he's not the chosen one either.' Jesse made seven of his sons pass before Samuel, but Samuel said, 'The Lord has not chosen any of these.' Finally, Samuel asked Jesse, 'Are all your sons here?' He answered, 'There is one more, the youngest, but he is out looking after the sheep.' Samuel said to Jesse, 'Send for him; we will not sit down until he's here.' Jesse sent for him to be fetched in. He was handsome, with glowing cheeks and shining eyes. The Lord said, 'Get up, and anoint him; for this is the one.' So Samuel took the horn of oil, and anointed him in the presence of his brothers; and the spirit of the Lord came with power upon David from that day onwards. Samuel set off and returned to Ramah.

Comment

If I were to ask you to draw a saint, what sort of picture would you come up with? The chances are it would be someone with a halo and an angelic smile. So how about if I asked you instead to draw a criminal – what then? In all likelihood it would be some shady-looking character wearing a mask and striped jersey, and carrying a swag bag over his shoulder!

Such are the stereotypical pictures we grow up with, and even though we may know they are not representative, we can find it very hard to shake such images off. The truth, of course, is that villains can appear all too plausible and presentable, just the sort of person we would trust, while, conversely, those who we might least expect, and who sometimes look anything but, can turn out to be unexpected saints. It's one thing, though, to know this in theory; another to put it into practice. Most, if not all of us, find it almost impossible to get beyond outward appearances – the youngster with the shaven head and Doc Marten boots whom we automatically label as a hooligan; the protestor whom we unconsciously tag as an extremist; the introvert whom we unthinkingly brand as aloof. Time and again, when it comes to making decisions, we judge by the outside.

So it was with Samuel, sent by God to anoint a successor to Saul as king of Israel. A simple enough task, so he imagined, and when Eliab, Jesse's eldest son was brought before him, he was convinced the job was as good as done. Why? Quite simply because Eliab looked the part – a young man with all the right outward credentials: tall, strong, handsome – and had the decision been left to Samuel it would have been Eliab rather than David who was anointed as successor to Saul. But he was in for a surprise; a word from God that was to question his whole way of thinking and expose the limitations of his judgement. As the New Revised Standard Version of the Bible puts it:

> The Lord said to Samuel, 'Do not look on his appearance or on the height of his stature, because I have rejected him; for the Lord does not see as mortals see; they look on the outward appearance, but the Lord looks on the heart.' (1 Samuel 16:7)

This is a reminder that God's ways are not our ways, nor his thoughts our thoughts, and implicit within that is a warning against judging others. We may think that we're a shrewd judge of character, the sort of person who can size someone up pretty quickly, but can we? Samuel found himself made to think again, to recognise that God looks beneath the surface to the person within. He alone knows each of us as we really are.

Here is a message that runs like a thread through the words and teaching of Jesus:

> Judge not, lest you be judged. For the way you judge others is the way you will be judged in turn, the treatment you hand out the treatment you will get back. Why is it you dwell on the speck in your neighbour's eye, when you can't even spot that log in your own? How can you say to others, 'Allow me to remove that speck from your eye, when all the time a log remains in your own eye?' You hypocrite, first remove the log from your own eye, and perhaps then you will see better to take the speck out of your neighbour's eye. (Matthew 7:1-5)

Do not judge by someone's face, but base your judgement on the things of God. (John 7:24)

Where others saw tax collectors and sinners, Jesus saw deeper. Where they looked at outward appearances and rejected, Jesus looked at the heart and accepted. Where we cast judgement, he offers forgiveness.

Do not judge others. Why? Because we will be judged in the same way ourselves? Yes. Because we are no better than others? Yes. But most of all simply because we have no way of seeing beneath the surface. We may think we are justified in our opinion of someone, that we know all we need to know about them, yet the truth is that we have no idea of their real feelings and motives. Only God can look into that secret place where 'I am really I'. Only God can finally judge. I have no doubt that Samuel learned that lesson. What about us?

Summary

- We all have built-in preconceptions and stereotyped images of right and wrong. These can subtly influence our decisions without us realising it.
- Samuel, a revered man of God, made the mistake of judging by the outside. Left to himself, he would have made the wrong decision as a result.
- Like Samuel, we too tend to judge by appearances.
- Jesus looked beneath the surface to the person beyond. Repeatedly he saw good in people where others saw only evil.
- We are never in a position to judge others. There is invariably more to a situation than meets the eye.
- It is vital to look beyond superficial impressions before making up our minds about anything. We need God's help to overcome the prejudices that colour our attitudes and distort our decisions.

Discussion

- The writings of Mary Ann Cross (née Evans) would probably have been lost for ever but for one thing – a change of name. Under the pseudonym George Eliot, Mary was to become one of the most celebrated English novelists of all time, her works including such classics as *Middlemarch*, *The Mill on the Floss* and *Silas Marner*. In similar fashion, the French novelist Aurore Dupin was to change her name to George Sand. Both knew that the only hope they had of being given a fair hearing was to conceal their true gender. Such were the prejudices faced by women in nineteenth-century society. What does this say to us about superficial impressions and the power of prejudice?

- Are there moments when you have been guilty of misjudging someone? What factors led you to jump to the wrong conclusions in the first place, and what led you to reassess your initial impressions? What have you learned from your experience?

- Do the labels society puts on people colour our judgement when meeting them? Do we label people, and, if so, in what ways?

- In what ways do prejudice and discrimination still have a hold in your life? Think about it honestly before rushing to answer.

- We do not only judge *people* by appearances; we can do just the same with situations and everyday items. How often have we been taken in by glossy advertising or attractive presentation?

- Recall moments when there was more to a situation than first met the eye. What made you look deeper? What lessons did you learn?

Meditation

It looked delicious –
   ripe,
   succulent,
   appetising –
so I took a bite . . .

and spat it out in disgust.
I should have known better, of course;
  should have learned by then
  that appearances aren't everything,
  yet, somehow, the message never seems to get through.
It's almost as though we can't help ourselves,
  a pleasant exterior all it takes to win us over,
  and when what's underneath
  fails to measure up to our expectations
  we express surprise,
  dismay,
  even anger,
  scarcely able to conceal our disbelief.
Lord, it may not matter much with fruit,
  but it does when it comes to people –
  when we're duped by outward show
  and taken in by a pretty face,
  when our attitudes are coloured by superficial impressions
  and we presume to pass judgement
  on what we do not understand.
Lord, help us to see not with our eyes but yours,
  and to catch a glimpse behind the façade,
  to the person within.

Further reading
Luke 11:37-41; Romans 14:10-13

Suggestions for action
Reflect on the opinions you have formed about people and the prejudices which may have coloured your judgement. Examine the reasons behind these and ask yourself whether it's time you thought again.

Prayer

Gracious God,
    we know how foolish it is to judge by the outside,
    yet time and again we catch ourselves doing it.
Our minds say one thing,
    but our hearts tell us another.
Even when we think we are looking deeper,
    we are still conditioned to look at the world in a set way,
    deceived by superficial impressions,
    failing to see the good in some
    and the evil in others.
Help us to see with your eyes,
    to look beyond the obvious
    to the deeper realities of life,
    and to recognise the true worth
    of all those around us.
Amen.

Fifth week of Lent
Living with decisions

Prayer

God grant me
the serenity to accept the things I cannot change,
the courage to change the things I can,
and the wisdom to know the difference.
Amen.

Unknown

Introduction

I wish I hadn't done that. How often have you spoken or thought along those lines? A careless word or a thoughtless action and we are left regretting our foolishness, wishing there was some way we could put the clock back and have another go at things. As the old saying has it, 'Act in haste, repent at leisure.' Yet, if there's truth in those words, there's truth also in another equally well-known saying: 'It's no good crying over spilt milk.' Like it or not, what's done is done, for better or for worse, and it's up to us to make the best of it. Learning to live with the consequences of our decisions is a necessary part of growing up.

Not, of course, that it's only our mistakes we can regret. We may equally have second thoughts about bold decisions taken on impulse that, in the cold light of day, look somewhat less appealing. They may be right, they may be admirable, but they may also be distinctly disturbing! That job we agreed to take on: can we really do it? That stand we resolved to make: have we the courage to see it through? That gift we promised: can we actually afford it? That responsibility we accepted: have we the necessary qualities to measure up to the challenge? We may feel, having agonised over a decision and finally made up our minds, that we've done all we need to do. The reality may turn out to be very different.

Activity

Estimation, Blob, Rage (see page 48).

Reading: Matthew 26:26-35

As they were eating, Jesus took a loaf and, having blessed it, he broke it and gave it to the disciples, saying, 'Take, eat, this is my body.' Then, taking a cup and giving thanks, he gave it to them, saying, 'Drink from it, all of you; this is my blood, the blood of the covenant, poured out for many for the forgiveness of sins. I tell you, I will not drink of this fruit of the vine again until that day when I drink it new with you in my Father's kingdom.' Then, after singing a hymn, they went out to the Mount of Olives.

Then Jesus said to them, 'You will all distance yourselves from me tonight; for it is written, "I will strike the shepherd, and the sheep of the flock will be scattered." But after I have been raised, I will go before you to Galilee.' Peter said to him, 'Though everyone else may forsake you, I never will!' Jesus said to him, 'Truly I tell you, you will disown me tonight three times, before the cock crows.' Peter protested, 'Even if I have to die for you, I will not disown you!' And all the disciples said the same.

Comment

There wasn't far to go. The climb had been long and steep but the end was in sight – just a short stretch and we'd be there. At least, that's what we thought, until we reached the brow of the hill and there, rearing up before us was another, a climb more demanding than the one we'd just completed. Decisions can be like that sometimes, can't they? We wrestle long and hard with a difficult problem and fondly imagine, once the decision is taken, that our problems are over, only to find that they've scarcely begun. Deciding can actually be the easy part; it's sticking to the choice we've made that can provide the stiffest test.

So it was to prove for the Apostles and, above all, for Peter. We've heard the story so many times before, yet it never fails to speak to us, for in Peter we catch a glimpse of ourselves. As we saw earlier in this series, he had made his decision, confessing his faith and declaring his commitment to Christ, but the signs were there even then that he'd failed to understand what following Jesus truly meant. Now the scenario is repeated – a different context but the same underlying misapprehension. 'Though everyone else may forsake you, I never will!' Were these just empty words, mere bravado? Of course not! Peter meant everything he said, and no doubt was convinced he would honour his promise. He'd made his choice and he intended to stick by it, come what may.

Events, as we know, were to prove him wrong, those words returning to haunt him as three times he denied knowing Jesus, just as had been predicted. The decision to follow had seemed easy enough so long as nothing was asked of him, but when the implications started to unfold, when commitment threatened to prove costly, then it was a different matter. Not that we should single out Peter especially, for the others fared no better, each of them to abandon Jesus in turn; and which of us in their place would have shown ourselves any more faithful? We can all start the journey of discipleship, but can we see it through?

In would be easy, in view of all this, to lose heart, but stop for a moment and consider the example of Jesus. He too, during that time in the wilderness, had made his decision and, for three years, he'd resolutely followed his chosen course. Despite hostility and ridicule, accusations of blasphemy and threats against his life, he'd stayed true to his calling, refusing to countenance any other way.

Yet, for one fleeting moment, in the Garden of Gethsemane, we get another picture, a compelling reminder of the humanity of Christ: 'He threw himself on the ground and prayed, "My Father, if it is possible, let this cup pass from me."' For Jesus, too, there came that awful moment when he had to face the consequences of the decisions he'd taken, and for him it was no easier than for us. Yes, unlike us he took the right way, but he understands how hard that can be, how difficult we find it to honour our commitment.

For Peter, failure wasn't the end of the story, nor for any of the other Apostles. They were given the opportunity to start afresh, the slate wiped clean, the past put behind them, and eventually, when the question was put to them again, they were not found wanting. For us too it is the same. We may find we have bitten off more than we can chew. We may repeatedly go back on the decisions we have made, unable to live up to our promises. We may find the implications of discipleship far more demanding than we ever anticipated and wonder just what it is that we've got ourselves into. Yet, however often we may fail, the invitation is always there to begin again, not alone but with Christ by our side. With his help we will find the strength we need to live with our decisions.

Summary

- Sometimes, having made a decision, we may wonder if we have done the right thing.
- Sticking to the choices we have made can be hugely costly and the temptation to compromise often proves hard to resist.
- Like Peter, we may find it impossible to live up to the decisions we have made.
- Failure to do so, however, is not the end. The unswerving faithfulness of Jesus to his calling means that we can find forgiveness and a fresh start. God is always ready to give us another chance.
- Through his Spirit, God will give us strength as we strive to honour the decisions we've taken.

Discussion

- A friend of mine was unhappy in her job but, after much heart searching, decided to stay on and make the best of things. She has regretted that decision to this day. Another friend, in a similar position, took the plunge and began a study course at home. For several years it was a long and demanding road, but today he is a partner in a flourishing business and thoroughly enjoying his work. What issues arise from their experience?

- Have there been times when you've regretted a decision? Why?

- Are there decisions you have found hard to live with but which you're none the less glad you took? What helped you get through the difficulties you faced?

- Have you ever wondered what you've taken on in committing your life to Christ? What do you find hardest about Christian discipleship? Are there ways in which your faith is all show and no substance?

- When you are conscious of commitment starting to waver, where do you turn to for support? What have you found most helpful in giving you strength to continue?

Meditation

It seemed a good idea at the time, Lord;
    not just the right thing to do, but the only thing.
You called
    and I responded,
    freely,
    thankfully,
    gladly,
    the joy of your love flooding my soul,
    the promise of new life stretching out gloriously before me.

I'd made my decision
  and I was happy to have done so,
  confident of the way ahead.
Only then the doubts started,
  not about you, but me,
  my ability to honour the promise I'd made.
It wasn't that my love changed, don't think that;
  simply that I began to understand
  what commitment involves.
Your call to love and go on loving,
  to give and go on giving,
  to turn the other cheek,
  forgive my enemies,
  walk the extra mile –
  I hadn't bargained on those,
  and, together, they've made me realise
  that taking a decision is one thing,
  living up to it quite another.
I'm scared, Lord,
  afraid of letting you down,
  of saying one thing and doing another,
  my faith all show and no substance.
I want to follow, you know that –
  but I'm not sure I have the courage or dedication I need
  to see it through.
Oh Lord, what have I done?
Where am I going?
You helped me decide,
  now help me live with my decision!

Further reading

Matthew 24:3-14; John 21:15-19; Hebrews 11:32-12:2

Suggestions for action

Identify areas in your life where you've gone back on your decision to follow Jesus. Resolve to do something about it and ask God for his help. Look for an opportunity this week to put your faith into practice, offering your time, your money, or your gifts in the service of others.

Prayer

Lord Jesus Christ,
    we have responded to your love
    and committed ourselves to your service,
    but we find it difficult sometimes
    to follow as we would wish,
    hard to live up to the faith we profess.
You bring us joy and fulfilment,
    but you bring also a disturbing challenge,
    calling us to a way of life that can be costly and demanding,
    such that we wonder sometimes quite what we've taken on.
By ourselves, we know we shall fail,
    so we come to you,
    bringing our weakness,
    our flawed commitment,
    our hesitant discipleship
    and ask for your strength
    to help us finish what we've started.
Reach out in love,
    and walk with us to our journey's end,
    for we ask it in your name.
Amen.

Activities

———— *Leaders' preparation notes* ————

Week One

Play a game of Jenga, Kerplunk or Matchsticks – i.e. any game in which participants take it in turns to remove a stick or tile without disturbing any of the others (or, in the case of Kerplunk, without dislodging any marbles). Discuss the issues/difficulties involved in coming to a decision as to which tile, stick or match to move.

Week Two

In advance of the session, choose two obscure words from the dictionary and write out three brief definitions for each (one true, and two false), as in the television quiz show *Call My Bluff.* Ask three members of the group (chosen and prepared before the meeting) to stage a couple of informal rounds. Invite the remaining members of the group to select the right answer. Discuss the difficulties involved in coming to a decision.

Alternatively, you might like to play a round of the board game Scruples (in which participants imagine themselves faced with a moral dilemma and have to decide which action to take); or stage a round of the balloon game, in which participants have to come up with a reason why they should be kept in the balloon. Discuss the issues involved in choices taken. Explore what the Christian perspective on each one might be.

Week Three

Borrow three small Lego packs (the sort tailored to create a particular model) and, dividing into three groups, give each five minutes to make something of the pieces. Do not tell them or show them what it is they are meant to be making. Encourage each group to work as a team. After the five minutes is up, invite the groups to display their creations. Next, give group members copies of the instructions and give them three minutes to build the specified model. Discuss the difference between following the maker's instructions and going it alone. (Whilst on this subject, you might like to share experiences of constructing MFI furniture!) How, if at all, do the issues here relate to life and faith?

Week Four

Show the group some pictures of everyday objects viewed from unusual angles, or of optical illusions (for example, the classic 'vase or two faces' picture). Explore together how easily appearances can be deceptive.

Week Five

Play a hand of the card game Estimation (also known as Blob or, in a slightly amended version, Rage). Playing by the basic rules of whist, each participant has to specify the number of tricks they expect to win before the game starts. After the hand is finished, discuss how difficult it was for each player to live with the decision they had taken. What factors complicated matters? How might this relate to life in general?